THE RAILWAYS OF CASTLEFORD

Normanton and Methley

By
C. T. Goode

Cover: *B1 No. 61131 draws a long freight working through Castleford on 24/7/65.*
R. G. Rockett

ISBN 1 870313 10 0
72 Woodland Drive, Anlaby, Hull. HU10 7HX.

Designed, Printed and Bound by
Swannack Brown & Co. Ltd.,
13a Anlaby Road, Hull.

Contents

Foreword

Castleford- who wants to write anything about Castleford? Thus did some folk respond when I dared to suggest a little railway book on the district, and yet such is perhaps needed and is possibly too late in some respects, as up to now no picture of the Lancachire & Yorkshire station at Methley Junction has been found, nor has any movement of steam - hauled passenger traffic been recorded on the L & Y, as far as can be discovered. Of course, what often happens is that a work of this kind has to be published before somebody writes in to say that a rich hoard of old prints has been found-would they be of any use, or is it to late?

Castleford-not a bad place really, home of a good rugby team and a spot which improves with visiting. There is a pleasant park, a rather blank and dominating new brick building between the river and railway bridge which is impressive but which remains anonymous, and an old library building which is full of life and crammed with books. Lots of the old industry has now gone, leaving the customary open spaces, though I was delighted to see a Burberry factory not far from the railway line.

I should like to thank Mr. Goodchild of Wakefield Library and Miss Ann Farrington of Castleford Library for their kind assistance, also Ron. Rockett and Derek Vause for their help and encouragement along the way. I hope that the choice of photographs included, though limited, will prove an interesting one. Anyone with hidden hoards should get in touch!

C. Tony Goode.
Anlaby, Hull. 1991.

Roman Legiolium

Castleford has been a practical sort of place all its life, without much of the pretentious or decorative about it, and yet it has enjoyed a quiet importance throughout, in the first place because of its position at the confluence of the rivers Aire and Calder. North of these two the lands of long ago were tribal and somewhat gloomy, while to the east stretched inhospitable fenland and bog as far as the North sea. Here were the preserves of the Brigantes, Celts who were governed by their leader Venutius from the capital Isurium, the later Aldborough. The Romans strode north along Ermine Street, conquering as they came through Lincoln and turning inland somewhat to Doncaster, thus avoiding the rather soggy Isle of Axholme. From Doncaster the way ran straight along an elevated causeway to the Calder crossing which afforded contrasting views of hills on the west side and dismal swamp on the other. At Legiolium the ford was made and a camp was placed on a fine, elevated site near the joining of the rivers at the point where the parish church of Castleford now stands. This is now a newer, 19th. century version of the original 13th. century building, beneath which a Roman milestone and amounts of pottery were found. At the ford itself were unearthed fragments of tessellated pavement, lamps, querns used for milling and an altar. In Carlton Street an information board today gives much interesting information on Roman times here, including the fact that the remains of a fort of eight acres exist beneath the site of the present Leo's supermarket. No doubt the centurions and others would be very amused to see how things have turned out today.

Being military men, the Romans soon polished off the Brigantes, pressing forward along the road northwards which would lead them to Isurium, with York lying just a mile or two north east along a branch from Bramham, much as Ilkley lay off in the other direction. Petilius Cerealis was victorious in several battles, the final of these being the routing of the Brigantes at Grassington on some date after 80AD, after which the tribe ceased to pose a problem.

It may often be wondered why Castleford never attracted the extra social and commercial activity which might have been expected for a place set at a good river crossing, compared with, say, York or Doncaster. The chief factor was most likely the terrain, for whereas the last two mentioned enjoyed land which was well-drained and which stood a decent distance above the river banks. Castleford's site was dull, damp and flat, certainly not conducive to good building. Thus it was that Pontefract nearby became prosperous, sporting decent buildings, a market and later social airs and graces. The town was set on much higher land.

To the north east of Castleford was more high land which marked the other side of the valley, itself scored by a beck with, on one flank, the village of Great Preston and on the other the limestone hilltop settlement of

Kippax. Both places had large mansions reflecting the desirability of residence here, with family names at Kippax Hall which included the Baildons, Slingsbys and Medhursts. There was cornmilling hereabouts, and what is relevant to the present subject, a regular market at Kippax, Domesday 'Chipesch' which means 'market under the ash tree'. The old Saxon church had also a castle as its neighbour.

The area is not noted for being the birthplace of local men and women who have brought distinction upon themselves, though one Thomas de Castleford, a 14th. century Benedictine monk was a native of the place, while the more famous Admiral Martin Frobisher was born at nearby Altofts and married a young lady of Whitwood in 1591. In our own day lived the famous sculptor Henry Moore, a Castleford man born in July 1898.

The first industry in the area would be pottery, with tile and brick-making developing using the local clays. Products would be carried away from the area by river, then by the Aire & Calder canal both inland to the growing towns and cities or towards the new port of Goole for shipment round the coast. With the development of coal mining in the area this commodity was transported in the same way. Add to this the growth of chemical works utilising the by-products of coal and the beginning of a vast production of glass jars and bottles, of which at one time some 20 million were produced annually, and the industrial picture begins to take shape. At the beginning of the century Castleford numbered a population of 14,000 narrowly beating its neighbour Pontefract.

The early canal

The railway companies, in particular the Lancashire & Yorkshire and its antecedents, worked well with the canal, here the Aire & Calder, a sufficiently rare harmony of canal and rail to be worth a mention. The railway paid 7% on the outlay of sidings, wharves and a new station at the flourishing port of Goole, with the canal company eventually obtaining a thousand year lease. The two competitors were always wary of each other, however, with the canal lopping one third off the toll charges in the face of what the L & Y could offer for the transit of coal outward and of corn and other produce inward. The canal was run almost as a family concern, with the Bartholomews father and son as engineers. Son William was born in 1831 and shared the running of affairs with the Traffic Manager, John Hargreaves. In September 1855 tolls had to be reduced still further, due to the competition for carriage from the NER; however, a new agreement was signed which enabled them to be raised again. One heartening event for the canal was that, in 1857 the NER admitted that it had abandoned the carriage of goods traffic between Leeds and Hull. So

BARTHOLOMEWS AIRE & CALDER SYSTEM. 1875.

CANAL BOAT PROPULSION.

W. H. BAILEY

THE BARTHOLOMEW SYSTEM, AIRE AND CALDER CANAL.

32. The Bartholomew system at work (*above*) side view; (*below*) taking a corner

well did it manage its business. This had been moved along by steam tugs from 1831, and longer trains of barges had been navigated through the three extended locks at Pollington from 1860, Whitley in 1861 and Castleford in 1867, from 6-7 tubs to 9-10 in most cases. Telephone wires were erected along the banks of the canal in 1861, in exchange for the free use of the system by the company.

At this time Bartholomew offered his Patent No. 330 which greatly improved the efficiency of load shipment and which was a worthy innovation. It dealt with a compound, articulated vessel made up of separate compartment boats close coupled with a bow compartment in front and a steering compartment at the rear. This was the forerunner of the pusher tugs, of which the best examples are those which propel huge loads along the Rhine and Moselle rivers today.

The inventor states: 'The steering of the compound vessel is to a great extent effected by chains or other connections which pass along each side of the compound vessel from stem to stern, each attached at one end to one of the terminal barges and at the other way they are passed around a capstan or windlass at the other extremity of the compound vessel, and

Good business awaits an incoming train headed by a G5, probably bound for the Kippax branch.   *Castleford Library*

the chains or connections are passed through suitable guides on each of the intermediate barges. By turning the capstan or windlass, the chain on one side of the compound vessel is wound up, and the chain on the other side is slacked out to a corresponding extent, and thus the compound vessel is drawn into a curved form, each barge pivoting about its projecting cutwater.'

In brief, each unit was 20 feet by 15 feet, a sort of amphibious railway truck with watertight doors at the sides or bottom for discharging on land. These were known as 'pans' at the Goole end of the canal, but 'Tom Puddings' inland. A hoist was installed at Goole to deal with unloading, and 3 mph. could be reached en route with a train of 168 tons. Initially each tub held 25 tons, which was later increased to 40 tons, while the maximum propelled load was up to 12 tubs. After 1890 a change of policy meant that the tug took the head of the train with a false bow behind it to dissipate the wake and then up to as many as 30-40 compartments. These would be divided, of course, for passage through the locks, though these were extended to become 215ft. by 22 ft. by 9 ft. as at Kippax.

The railway was also improving its position, chiefly by the opening of the NER line from Thorne Jc. to Staddlethorpe through Goole, which allowed the Manchester, Sheffield & Lincolnshire Railway to send its South Yorkshire coal to Goole and Hull at cheaper rates, a fact which affected the Aire & Calder once more, though it was well able to fight back with good loading facilities, particularly in the arrangement at Stanley basin where St. John's colliery at Normanton hauled out the tubs from the water by steam engine and then ran them on a railway for $1^{1}/_{2}$ miles to the colliery for loading and return to canal. The idea was a success, with the basin enlarged in 1898. The outfit ran until its closure in 1941.

After 1870 grain traffic from the eastern side of England fell off, due to cheaper American imports through Liverpool, whereas the shipment of coal more than doubled between 1851 and 1870. There were also growing imports of timber. Problems of operation included great frosts of 1893 and 1895, and the opening of the Hull & Barnsley Railway in 1885 which provided another route for South Yorkshire coal to Hull.

First railway schemes - Normanton

With the canal nicely established, the railway development tended to follow this and the river valleys for ease of construction, a policy which often left it somewhat apart from centres of population which might be profitably served; thus, both Castleford and Pontefract missed the main tide of progress, as did Wakefield initially, lying as it does on higher ground. The first major railway to pass through the district was the North Midland from Derby to Leeds (Hunslet Lane) which received its Act on

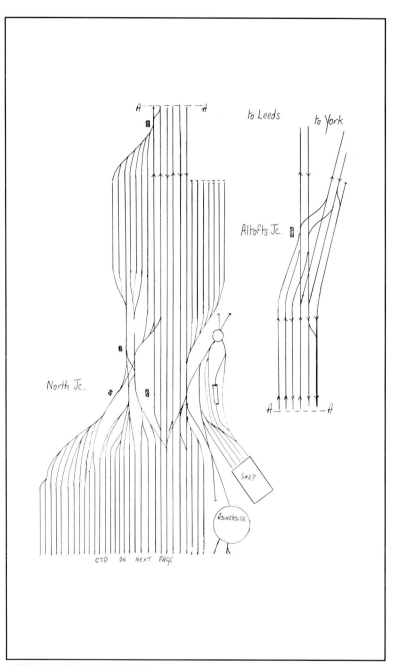

NORMANTON STATION AREA

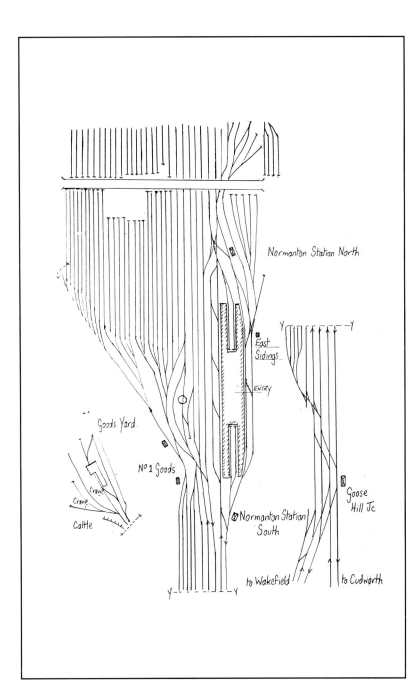

Normanton Station North

East Sidings

ENTRY

Goods Yard

No 1 Goods

Crane

Crane

Cattle

Normanton Station South

Goose Hill Jc

to Wakefield

to Cudworth

An unidentified 'Compound' enters Normanton with a Sheffield local. The loco. depot and cooling tower are in the background. 1951   *C. T. Goode*

4th. July 1836 and ran from Masborough (Rotherham) up through Methley, the nearest point to Castleford, keeping to low ground and using George Stephenson's ruling gradient of 1 in 330.

There was much afoot on the railway scene at this time, and a remarkable amount of co-ordination of opening dates on a level which would certainly not be met with nowadays. The Manchester & Leeds Railway was beavering away to the west and came down the Calder valley via Mirfield, reaching the NMR at Goose Hill Jc. and providing train services between Manchester and Leeds from 1841.

In this part of the world it was becoming logical in some quarters to consider Leeds as the focal point of developing railways, though for George Hudson the only real contender was York, at the south end of his Great North of England Railway and, though a worthy place, really too far east to be effective. However, Hudson was Chairman of another company, the York & North Midland, and on 26th. June 1836 this letter received its Act to open a new line in three stages, from York to a junction with the little Leeds & Selby Railway at York Jc., also called Old Jc. and later Gascoigne Wood on 29th. May 1839, then a stage from Sherburn Jc. to Burton Salmon on 11th. May 1840 and finally from Burton Salmon to Altofts Jc. on the NMR on 30th. June 1840. The latter neatly coincided with opening of the NMR between Goose Hill Jc. and Altofts Jc., a run of two or three miles, flat and uninviting which was shared with Altofts Hall, and what better place to create a useful railway junction and marshalling yards and to call it Normanton? Normanton village did exist in 1840, with 280 souls, a number which had grown to 481 by the following year and to 12,300 by the end of the century; such was the growth of the beast. In November 1840 a fine station was opened, in Italian villa style, financed by three companies but managed by the NMR. The hand of the NER architect G.T. Andrews was evident. Finishing touches were put in hand and completed by September 1841 and a hotel and refreshment rooms were opened the following year, connected to the station proper by a covered way. The 'Railway Times' in 1844 made the telling comment that at Normanton porters were rude to all passengers as a matter of course, especially those using M & L trains, while single females were put in a state of near hysteria. The place was an early watering hole or service area in today's parlance, for express services between the north and Euston via Masborough, Derby and Rugby. Things were going so well that, by 1849 the Midland, as the North Midland had now become, had decided to enlarge the station, though some gilt fell off the gingerbread when other, easier routes were opened in due course such as the London & North Western's Manchester to Leeds via Huddersfield and the NER

Methley Jc. L & Y line to left, NE Whitwood curve off between hut and signal box. Joint station in background on embankment.   *J. P. Wilson*

13

Part of the island platform at Normanton. 1960.   C. T. Goode

Leeds to Thirsk. The idea of using Normanton as a refreshment stop persisted on the opening of the Settle & Carlisle route to Scotland in 1876, with a further rebuilding of the premises from two islands to one vast central island of one quarter of a mile in length. The local fug, however, did little for the beauty of the buildings thereon. The refreshment rooms now catered for passengers who wished to order food ahead of them down the line, rather as is still met with on Indian railways. On notification at Sheffield and within half an hour or so a five course meal could be prepared, ready and waiting, a feat which pointed to a skilled, plentiful and dedicated staff. All this activity dwindled and vanished on the introduction of dining cars in 1895, after which Normanton became more important for the exchange of letters and parcels run by a joint MR/NER service between Bristol and Newcastle. A Travelling Post Office would also leave St. Pancras, be attached at Derby and latter removed at Normanton for Leeds and, ultimately Carnforth. Another working with early antecedents was the mail from Bangor which first ran in 1855 and went via Crewe, Stockport and Stalybridge, terminating at Normanton, the service operating regularly until 1902.

Today Normanton is a 'bus stop' on the area network of dmus, with the vast island somewhere beneath a small plantation of laurel bushes.

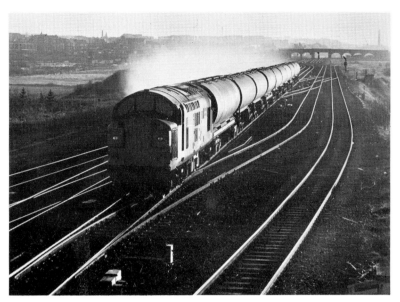

Taken from Altofts Jc. signal box, No. 37077 passes with a Stanlow - York train on 25/1/86. S. Batty

Lines to Selby

At this point we can introduce the Leeds & Selby Railway, an innocuous and independent little concern which formed part of the overall idea of a line which would run from Liverpool eastwards towards Hull. Selby was a useful division at the place where the Ouse flowed through, and a terminal station was sited here with facilities for Hull passengers to connect with the river steamer. The line was begun on 1st. October 1830 and opened for traffic on 22nd. September 1834, following surveys conducted by George Stephenson and James Walker. Originally the L & S was unconnected with other railways, but, as we have seen it soon encountered Hudson's Y & NM line which crossed it at right angles en route to Normanton, opening to York Jc. on 29th. May 1839. The Leeds & Selby was indeed a thorn in the side of both the NMR and Y & NM, with the former wanting a share of the Hull traffic and suggesting trains run alternately with those of the L & S, an idea with which the little company could not agree. Hudson, for the Y & NM realised that though this proposal was only a slight one, any competition at all would be undesirable and so decided to gain control of the L & S, with the latter's directors agreeing to lease their railway to the Y & NM for 31 years for a

15

rental of £17,000. The lease took effect from 9th. November 1842 and the L & S was promptly closed to passenger traffic between Leeds Marsh Lane, the first terminus and Old (York) Jc., the reason given that the Leeds site was remote and that connections with other trains could not be made, both of which were expedient but true. There was also the option of purchasing the line for £210,000, a course which was eventually taken.

Passengers between Hull and Sheffield could change at Sherburn Jc., while on 29th. July 1840 the Y & NM curve from Whitwood Jc. to Methley Jc. on the North Midland was opened and a direct York-Leeds service was run this way for the next 29 years. Methley station was opened north of the junction on the NMR (Methley North) and was well sited in the village. On 9th. November 1840 a new south-east curve from Old Jc. to Milford Jc. was opened and the transfer of Hull passengers who could now enjoy rail travel all the way, was moved to the latter place instead of Sherburn Jc.

The crossing of the Leeds & Selby was interesting historically, with the original York Jc. reopening in December 1850 as Old Jc., then known as Milford Old Jc. from 1867. The junction then became Gascoigne Wood from 1879 and the spot remained open as a passenger halt until 1902. Following the setting up of a small yard here the halt was reopened in 1907 for staff purposes, disappearing when the yard closed on 2nd. November 1859. Round the corner to the south Milford Jc. remained open until 1st. October 1904, with the station buildings surviving tenuously until they were demolished, this in October 1960. During the period of excursion trains on summer Saturdays both places were used for crew and engine changing purposes between Midland and NE area workings; some rather curious arrangements of motive power were to be seen here, ranging from 'Royal Scots' to Class D 20s in tandem.

The Whitwood-Methley Jc. curve initially offered a competitive route to Leeds from Selby, even though it was 4½ miles longer; however, it was more pleasant to travel through in one train rather than change at Milford. Freight was diverted off the L & S through Methley from July 1948, though local traffic did in fact reappear again after two years had passed. On 1st. April 1869 the new link running west to north from Micklefield to Church Fenton was opened, along with Leeds New station, and the need for the Whitwood curve largely vanished as the passenger services over its whole length ceased.

- and to Goole

Following the establishment of the Aire & Calder navigation and the successful growth of Goole as a port dealing in coal and corn, various railway promoters were attracted and up to four schemes were proposed to strengthen the commercial links, these being the Barnsley & Goole,

Goole & Doncaster and Brayton & Goole, all of which failed, though the latter, a Y & NM project, did appear in a modified form later on. The fourth, the Wakefield, Pontefract & Goole Railway, was successful and was in essence a junction with the M & L at Wakefield, then a run through Pontefract and Knottingley to Goole. At a meeting in Pontefract in 1844 it was stressed how much corn passed through Goole inland from the eastern countries to Wakefield, at that time a large market, how much coal passed the other way from the mines in the Wakefield area, the importance of Pontefract as an agricultural centre and the lime quarries at Knottingley. Such persuasive argument stirred the Board of Trade, though not the principal companies such as the NM and Y & NM, as George Hudson was heartily opposed to the proposal. The M & L put up half of the capital required and appointed five directors. Construction was awarded to a Wakefield man, Joseph Thornton, with John Harris as the engineer. Estimate for the total cost of the new line was £365,000, and after the line was leased to the M & L it was soon amalgamated with them, while at about the same time, on 9th. July 1847 the company name was changed to the Lancashire & Yorkshire Railway. By an Act of 16th. July 1846 three further branches were authorised, including that from Pontefract to the NMR at Methley which would offer access over that line to Leeds, and a branch from Knottingley to Askern north of Doncaster

An outline view of a Class 141 unit on the 15.01 Knottingley to Leeds at Whitwood. 6/12/84. S. Batty

17

which would allow the Great Northern access to these lines from the south via Shaftholme Jc. Joseph Thornton had, once again, the contract for the Methley line, or rather the south-eastern half of it, with the rest going to Messrs. Pearson & Woodhouse. The line was planned to open on 3rd. September 1849, to coincide with the GNR line from Retford to Doncaster, though first trains to run were the St. Leger race specials on 12th. September with an opening for regular services from 1st. December. The L & Y provided a passenger service between Leeds and Methley Jc. from 1st. April 1850, while the GNR used its running powers to offer a service between Doncaster and Leeds. These trains went by way of Methley until 1st. January 1866 when the joint GN and MS & L line from Doncaster to Wakefield Westgate was opened. This, in turn, connected with a joint operation by the L & Y and GN from Wakefield to Leeds Central, gained by a spur from Kirkgate station in Wakefield, round to Westgate. The latter was opened on 3rd. October 1857 and was used by some L & Y and GN trains. Castleford L & Y station was opened in 1860. M & L trains began to run via Methley to Leeds Hunslet Lane from 1st. March 1841, using the new route from Manchester through Todmorden and Wakefield and by running powers from Goose Hill Jc. through Normanton.

The Great Northern played a not inconsiderable part in the railway scene at Methley, due to their being chiefly hell-bent on completing a main route from London to the North. An Act was passed on 26th. June 1846 known as the London & York Act which contained proposals for branches to Leeds and Wakefield which were in fact not accepted. However, at the same time the Askern-Methley Jc. proposal of the WP & GR was accepted and the GN took the opportunity of reaching Leeds by this route. The Midland (former NMR) was somewhat disturbed by the proposal and sought to block it by suggesting its own Leeds, Wakefield & Midland Junction Railway from Chevet to Rothwell, a shorter route than that via Methley. This was rejected and the GN was allowed to go ahead under contract to use the WP & G lines from Askern Jc. to Wakefield and Methley Jc. The MR chipped in with running powers granted to GN locomotives and stock from Methley to Leeds, the agreement signed by George Hudson himself on 16th. October 1847.

The Knottingley to Askern Jc. section of what was now the L & YR was opened on 6th. June 1848, with the GN 'bit' from Askern Jc. to Stocksbridge (Arksey) on the following day. This, in turn, was followed by the Arksey to Doncaster section in August. It was hoped that the L & Y line to Methley Jc. would be open on 3rd. September 1849, so that a Peterborough to Leeds service might be operated; however, this was thwarted because of a dispute between the GNR and MR-there was a similar one at Nottingham-known as 'the Methley incident'. This seems to have arisen because the GN refused to give an undertaking never to construct a line of its own to Leeds, whereupon the MR proposed to stop all GN trains at Methley and charge tolls for the passengers. If the 'Doncaster Chronicle' of the day is correct in its report, then passengers were not considered to be of much account in the affair:

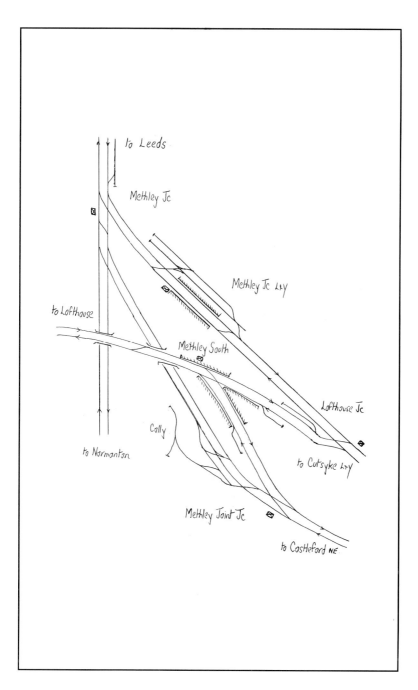

to Leeds

Methley Jc

Methley Jc Lry

to Lofthouse

Methley South

Lofthouse Jc

Cally

to Cutsyke Lry

to Normanton

Methley Joint Jc

to Castleford NE.

'Atrocious conduct in a railway company', so ran the headline. 'The Superintendent at Doncaster, having heard it whispered that something was going on at the junction of the Doncaster line with the Midland at Methley, sent over a special engine before the trains and found that the servants of the Midland company had removed the points at the junction, so that had the train proceeded, it would have inevitably run off the road.'

The GNR remained wary of the MR for some time and worked St. Leger traffic to Leeds via Wakefield and Normanton, working with the L & Y where necessary. The Methley route was fully in use from 1st. October 1849, being officially open from 1st. December and with the L & Y Goole-Leeds trains in action from 1st. April 1850. The L & Y station at Castleford was hardly in the centre of things, being set out to the west of the town and without any goods facilities. The station enjoyed an L & Y service between Knottingley and Leeds from 1860.

L & Y traffic for Hull had originally been worked by way of Normanton and Selby, following an agreement with Hudson of 1846, and when the branch built by the NER from Thorne to Staddlethorpe opened in October 1869, an easier route was available through Goole.

Great efforts were made by the L & Y to secure the race traffic to Doncaster, and excursions were advertised from Leeds and as far away as Manchester Victoria.

At its peak, traffic through Methley Jc. was run by four different companies, the Midland, L & Y, Y & NM and GN. However, this euphoric state of affairs did not last long, as the L & Y services between Manchester and Leeds went by a quicker route from 1st. August 1854 when the line from Bowling Jc. to Leeds Central was opened and trains took a shorter route via Milner Royd Jc. and Halifax. GN trains continued to run as mentioned until the opening of the West Yorkshire Railway from Wakefield via Lofthouse and Ardsley to Leeds on 3rd. October 1857, with the commencment of long distance trains on 1st. November. These ran by way of Pontefract and Wakefield, still utilising one of the L & Y lines through Knottingley.

The GN makes its mark

The Y & NM became the North Eastern Railway from 1854, and in due course the company sought to obtain a better route between Leeds and York. To this end the old L & S line was extended from Marsh Lane to Leeds New station which was built jointly with the LNWR and opened in 1865, the line actually running beyond to connect with the MR at Leeds Jc. Further afield to the east a new 'cut-off' line was put in from Micklefield round northwards to Church Fenton which gave a much shorter and more acceptable run to York and removed the need for these services to pass

Lofthouse Jc. looking towards Methley. Feb. 1981. Latterly this box was opened only when required by coal trains coming from Newmarket Colliery. It suffered badly from vandals and a set of wooden shutters was provided to protect the windows when the box was not occupied. R. G. Rockett

through Methley. This route was available from 1st. April 1869. The original Whitwood-Methley curve was used for some coal traffic up to about 1904. This move might have marked the end of the curve as far as passenger trains were concerned, had not a further local project entered the scene. This was embodied in the Leeds & Methley Railway Act of 21st. July 1863 to build a line running east from the West Yorkshire Railway, soon to be absorbed into the GNR, from a triangular junction at Lofthouse north of Wakefield through Stanley to Methley across the MR and dropping down between the L & Y Methley-Pontefract line and the Whitwood curve, to both of which connections were sent off at Lofthouse Jc. (L & Y) and Methley Joint Jc. (NER). At the point of division was Methley Joint station. The new line was known as the Methley Joint Railway, promoted by three companies, the GN, L & Y and NER, though in the style of the major interest, the GN who also provided the trains which began to run between Wakefield or Leeds to Castleford from 13th. May 1869. Goods traffic had begun in 1865 and the GN had running powers as far as Milford Jc. with freight from Bradford beginning on 8th. June 1866. A service of passenger trains ran between Bradford and York via Milford Jc. during the summer season of 1876-7. Lofthouse Joint station became Lofthouse, then Lofthouse & Outwood from July 1888. The

21

GN was allowed one third of receipts from working the passenger service, this being adjusted from 1st. January 1885 to one shilling per mile for all trains working on the branch.

Locally the line gave access to collieries at Lofthouse and Stanley. The south curve at Lofthouse enabled the running of the passenger service between Wakefield Kirkgate and Milford Jc. six of them on a somewhat circuitous route.

The Y & NM turned into the NER from 1854 and in due course the company sought to obtain a better route.

The line passed over some rather spongy terrain, especially at the Stanley end, and services were interrupted by flooding on 28th. January 1883 which caused single line working for a time. This happened again in 1892, following which the formation was raised by four feet along 500 yd. to alleviate the problem.

The MR which passed to the west of the Methley Joint line junctions and which was not affected by developments apart from its own junction at Methley proper, tried its hand at a Leeds-Castleford service from 1st. August 1869, no doubt as a counter-blast to the GN, the trains running to the remote station at Cutsyke. This was, however, discontinued after a

Methley Joint station looking west.   *J. P. Wilson*

short while and the company contented itself with the stopping trains at Methley North and Altofts on its own line, both stations within reasonable distance of Castleford. There was comparatively little colliery development around the L & Y line, except for that at Glasshoughton to the south of Castleford.

The NER arrives via Kippax

There were new developments in the coalfield to the north east of the town at Kippax, Ledston (sometimes Ledstone) and Allerton Bywater, and it was decided to obtain an Act and open the Leeds, Castleford & Pontefract Junction Railway, which was done in 1873. The route ran from Castleford north through the places mentioned to Garforth on the Leeds & Selby line which was approached by a west facing junction. The line was nominally independent but the NER owned three quarters of the capital and duly absorbed it in 1876. The line opened two years later with a local passenger service from 12th. August 1878, this running to Pontefract on the new Swinton & Knottingley Joint line from 1st. April 1880 after connections had been put in from Castleford NE round to Cutsyke Jc, on

Ledston Station. Looking north in 1960.   *P. Cookson*

23

Kippax Station. Looking south in 1960. Try counting the lighting!   P. Cookson

the L & Y and from Pontefract L & Y round to the new station at Baghill on what looked like an expensive and tall viaduct.

The line saw heavy coal traffic from the outset which was worked by the NER to Goole. However, from 1899 L & Y engines and men worked the trains. From 1st. November 1926 the Leeds-Pontefract passenger trains were cut back to Castleford only, presumably as an economy measure.

The original station at Castleford was rather cramped, on the enbankment at Bridge street at the east end of the town and in no way as convenient as the later, final version opened in 1871 south of the main centre of town activities. In LNER days during the thirties there was a drive to give passengers facilities with a more popular image, rather after the style of the Great Western who opened 'halts' all over the place prior to the Great War. With the LNER such platforms, often rudimentary wooden affairs, appeared at such places as Springhead (Hull), Penda's Way (Leeds) and Bowers north of Ledston on the Kippax branch, ostensibly to serve a housing estate, opening as a halt on 15th. December 1934, though in May 1937 the suffix 'halt' was removed.

How the railways affected matters

The topography of the lines round Castleford and Methley was interesting and quite intricate, and the author found initial difficulty in locating exactly what went where until the bits and pieces finally settled into place after two or three runs on the local dmus. Equally arduous were the ramifications of the passenger services, particularly the variants which

Castleford 'Old' station in the 1960s, shortly before demolition. Castleford Libraries

arose in early BR days around 1950. The North Eastern region with its orange totems and baby blue station seats-the painters have recently been back to Goole with supplies of the shade which they have obviously rediscovered-was always willing to try some new variations for a time. The Midland main line was the easy one, with its station at Methley North handling modest traffic until its closure on 16th. September 1957. Altofts & Whitwood to the south of Methley Jc. enjoyed similar traffic on its high embankment, but was closed eventually in 1990 due to re-routing of the local dmu service which gave it the cold shoulder.

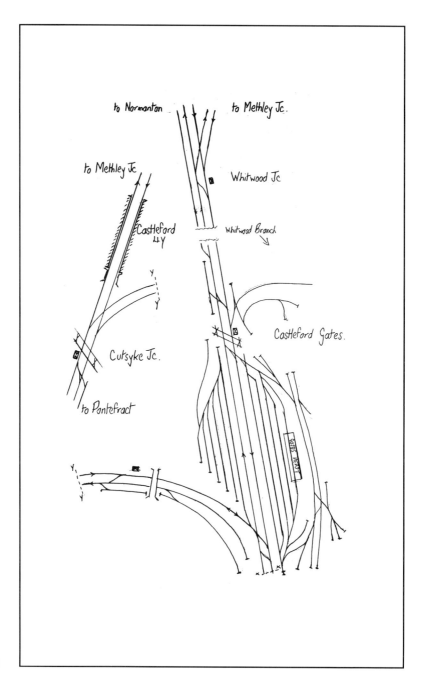

to Normanton   to Methley Jc.

to Methley Jc

Whitwood Jc

Castleford H Y

Whitwood Branch

Castleford Gates.

Cutsyke Jc.

to Pontefract

GOODS DEPOT

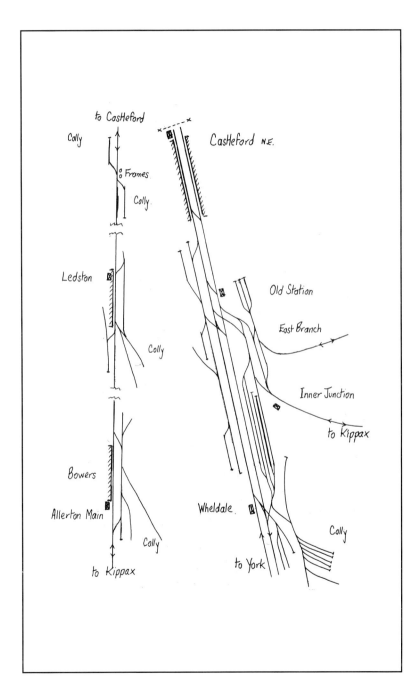

to Castleford

Colly

Castleford N.E.

Frames

Colly

Colly

Ledston

Old Station

East Branch

Colly

Inner Junction

to Kippax

Bowers

Wheldale

Allerton Main

Colly

Colly

to Kippax

to York

A B1 and J6 as pilot rest before (presumably) taking on an excursion at Castleford, probably over the heavier gradients round Bradford. R. G. Rockett

The Y & NM, later NER major route from Burton Salmon towards Normanton through Castleford Central enjoyed a full service of all kinds of traffic, with some local services terminating at Normanton, as did some local Midland trains. Generally the line persists, particularly for block loads of fuel oil. Burton Salmon station closed on 14th. September 1959. Gascoigne Wood was the first station in the area to close in 1902, with Milford Jc. following two years later. The Garforth-Castleford branch lost its passenger service on 22nd. January 1951 when the stations at Kippax and Ledston (without the final -e) closed, along with the LNER halt at Bowers situated adjacent to Allerton Main. Both Kippax and Ledston had substantial NER style brick buildings with a good crop of gas lamps on the platforms. It can be assumed that the passenger workings were often something of an embarrassment on a single line which was filled with mineral traffic ready to go. Garforth station buildings seem to have been preserved and the station remains an important source of revenue from commuter traffic on the Leeds-Selby-York lines.

It is interesting to note here that a development strategy for local railways around Leeds made provision for the use of the Kippax branch for a short distance at the north end, and included halts at Green Lane, Ninelands Lane and South Garforth, though nothing further has been

The Old station entrance at Castleford Bridge Street.   *Castleford Library*

heard of this particular scheme since the opening of a new halt at East
Garforth on the main line.

Methley South station 1958. Left hand line to Pontefract L & Y and Lofthouse Jc.
Right hand line to Castleford NE.   P. Cookson

Methley Joint Station

The GN trains on the Methley Joint line kept open the rather isolated
station of Methley South with its platforms set on each side of the Y
junction, although in fact there do not appear to have been any stopping
passenger services down to the L & Y at Lofthouse Jc., only to Castleford
Cen. over the southern portion of the Whitwood curve. The northern
portion, over which so much often controversial traffic had run in the early
days, soldiered on with the occasional goods train, being closed from
Methley Joint Jc. on 30th. June 1929 and the points taken out at Methley
Jc. (MR) in 1930-1. The remnant of line from the south end led to a
colliery only. Things were reinstated on 30th. July 1967 by BR in
connection with a new marshalling yard planned for Stourton, which never
materialised. Methley South station closed on 7th. March 1960. The new
diesel units entered the picture locally in 1954 running round Leeds,
Bradford and Harrogate districts, and they soon appeared on the Leeds-
Castleford service over the Methley Joint line from 5th. May 1958 with an
extended run to Pontefract. The service finished in 1964 when the Joint
line closed.

Methley South station. (MJR) looking west in 1958.   *P. Cookson*

The L & Y and Cutsyke

L & Y passenger services went about their business quietly, using Knottingley as a sort of focal point. The station here had been enlarged over the years, with an overall roof and had become something of an eyesore, a rusting and rotting hulk before it was cleared away in the 60s. Services ran to Doncaster and Askern, though these were cut back to Askern only after 10th. March 1947, just before the junction with the GN at Shaftholme, due to problems in fitting them in with the pace of the East Coast main line flyers. The other eastbound service was to Goole, while in the other direction trains ran to Leeds and Wakefield. In the area under review the two relevant stations were both on the Methley Jc. branch, at Castleford, known as Cutsyke after 1952, and Methley Jc., the latter being just at the point before the line joined the MR and fitting neatly into the space in a shallow cutting complete with a goods yard, the whole just below the Methley Joint station. Both served very little, except a row or two of cottages labelled Methley Jc. on the map. Methley Jc. L & Y is given in one reference as being closed from 1st. October 1904, probably for a time, but closure certainly took place during 1943.

As mentioned earlier, Cutsyke was at the wrong end of Castleford, and   31

Remains of Methley L & Y looking west in April 1955. The Midland line crosses the view in the background. *J. P. Wilson*

The collection of huts that was Cutsyke. *Castleford Library*

even if it existed today would only manage to serve the local swimming pool and hospital. There was a spartan arrangement of platforms on an embankment and no goods facilities.

The original idea of running NER Garforth-Castleford trains on to Pontefract via the spur round to Cutsyke Jc. on the L & Y was a handy one for later years, as it enabled dmus to use the ex NER station which was central in the town and to allow the section of the L & Y from Cutsyke Jc. to Methley Jc. to be closed, which did in fact happen in 1968 without the shedding of many tears. Before this happened, however, there was a Leeds-Knottingley dmu service which served Cutsyke and which was extended to Goole from 2nd. January 1967 as compensation for the loss of the Wakefield-Goole service, which in turn meant the closure of Sharlston and Tanshelf stations. Both these and a new one at Streethouse are due to reopen on a revitalised line in due course.

BR policy in recent years

With the closure of Cutsyke station in 1968 dmus ran into Castleford Central to reverse, using the restored Whitwood curve and out again to join the L & Y at Cutsyke Jc., a spur which had enjoyed its ups and downs,

Class 141 unit enters Castleford on 9.00 from Leeds 27/10/84. Note the vast emptiness of the railway scene.   *S. Batty*

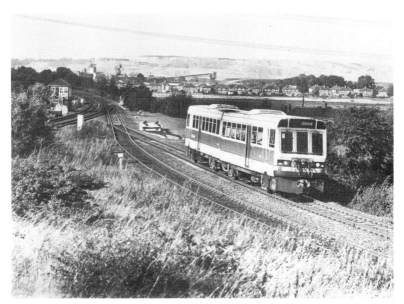

The 15.03 Leeds-Goole at Methley Jc. 24/9/85. The Midland main line curves left.
S. Batty

being initially opened on 1st. April 1880, then closed to passengers from 1st. November 1926, reopened on 5th. May 1958 to close again on 2nd. November 1964 and finally opening on 7th. October 1968 when the direct L & Y line was cut. Access to this spur from the NER proper was for a time somewhat unorthodox although the NER, whose property it was, did tend to go in for some peculiar pointwork in places. Here the line started as single, doubling up when round the curve once the line leading from the station yard had joined in, adjacent to a brickworks.

At this later period significant changes in the railway operating pattern in the area were the end of the York-Manchester passenger services via Wakefield Kirkgate in 1970 which were now concentrated on the LNW section through Huddersfield. The L & Y trains had brought in some of that company's engines including the Hughes 4-6-0s which performed until their ultimate withdrawal. Closure of the extensive yards at Normanton came in 1968 and also the closure of the Midland main line from Goose Hill Jc. down through Cudworth to Wath Road Jc., ostensibly due to mining subsidence en route. The line was reopened for a time during 1973 while the S & K Joint line had been adopted as the alternative Intercity route between Leeds and Sheffield.

Currently the hourly dmu service of local trains from Leeds to Sheffield

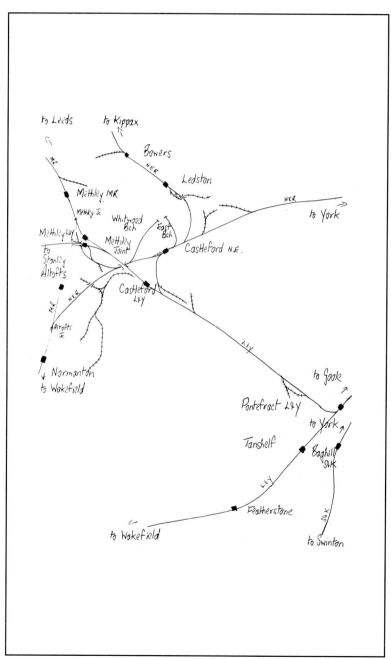

to Leeds   to Kippax

Bowers

NER

Ledston

Methley MR

MR

Methley Jc

Whitwood Bch

East Bch

Methley Joint

Methley L&Y

NER

to York

Castleford N.E.

to Stanley

Altofts

Castleford L&Y

MR   NER

Altofts Jc

Normanton
to Wakefield

L&Y

to Goole

Pontefract L&Y

to York

Tanshelf

Baghill S&K

L&Y

Featherstone

to Wakefield

S&K

to Swinton

RAILWAYS AT CASTLEFORD

via Barnsley is diverted to serve Castleford, running by way of the Whitwood spur to the station, then reversing and running to Altofts Jc. where the large signal box has lately been removed, regaining the normal stops from Normanton. Only Altofts & Whitwood station has suffered because of this manoeuvre. There is also a reasonable service to Knottingley, reversing at Castleford, thence on to the L & Y at Cutsyke, though only two trains each way daily make the run to Goole; at least this is 100% better than the single train which ran in 1956! (see page 59-61).

There was quite a rash of innovation during the early BR days of the fifties, with trains running between the most unlikely places such as Cleethorpes and Hastings. One such operation is recalled by the author as a through dmu service between Hull and Bradford Exchange around the 1958 period which he used but cannot for the life of him remember by which route it travelled, except that it stopped at Morley High on the way. Possibly the route taken would be via Selby, Burton Salmon, Castleford and the Methley Joint line as being the most direct. More information on this would be interesting.

Midland and L & Y local services

It is difficult to give a good picture of passenger train services in a given area, as to begin with a review could not cover a century and a half with out becoming tedious. However, some typical examples of what was on offer are given below, and it will be seen that there was a great deal of railway activity. Firstly the Midland local trains called at Methley, most of which would also serve Altofts & Whitwood:

Departures on weekdays from Methley to Leeds in 1914.

6.20am	from Normanton	Slow
7.25	starts	Slow
7.50	from Normanton	Slow
8.54	from Sheffield	Slow
1.42pm	from Barnsley	Slow
3.57 SO	from Normanton	Slow
4.17	from Chesterfield	Slow
6.01	from Sheffield	Slow
8.38	from Dore & Totley	Slow
9.30	from Sheffield	Semi-fast
10.21 SO	from Normanton	Slow

Departures from Methley on weekdays southbound in 1914.

6.48am	terminates	Slow

7.02	terminates	Slow
8.49	to Normanton	Slow
10.52	to Barnsley	Slow
12.41pm	to Barnsley	Slow
1.57	to Normanton	Slow
3.09	to Sheffield	Takes up only
4.56	to Chesterfield	Slow
6.55	to Barnsley	Slow
7.39	to Sheffield	Slow
9.02	to Barnsley	Slow
9.34 SO	to Normanton	Slow
10.32 SX	to Normanton	Slow
11.22	to Normanton	Slow
	(Tu.Th SO to Barnsley)	

Sundays

10.34am	Derby to Leeds	Slow
3.32pm	Sheffield to Leeds	Slow
8.19	Barnsley to Leeds	Slow
9.54	Derby to Leeds	Slow

No. 40077 tracklifting between Cutsyke and Lofthouse Jc. Sept 1982. R. G. Rockett

Compound No. 41050 pilots No. 73030 on a Bradford - Derby working at Methley Jc. 24/4/55. *J. P. Wilson*

7.27am	Leeds to Derby	Slow
2.19pm	Leeds to Derby	Slow
7.23	Leeds to Chesterfield	Slow
9.23	Leeds to Normanton	Slow

The L & Y had a neat service of trains with connections at Knottingley for Goole or Doncaster, also for Wakefield, though for simplicity these are not given here. The tables are for 1914. There was no Sunday service:

Leeds	dep:	9.10am	10.45	1.22pm	3.47	5.40	7.55	11.00SO
Methley MR	dep:	9.27	....	1.39	4.04	5.57	....	....
Methley Jc.	dep:	9.30	11.03	1.42	4.11	6.00	8.13	....
Castleford	dep:	9.33	11.07	1.45	4.14	6.03	8.16	11.18
Knottingley	dep:	9.43	11.18	1.55	4.26	6.14	8.26	11.34
Goole	arr:	10.19	11.56	2.40	5.10	6.55	9.08	12.11am
Doncaster	arr:	10.20	12.07	2.47	5.05	6.52	9.19	....

Doncaster	dep:	7.22am	9.00	11.00	1.35pm	4.00	....	6.04
Goole	dep:	7.20	8.57	11.05	1.40	3.55	2.27SO	5.55
Knottingley	dep:	7.49	9.26	11.34	2.11	4.25	2.58	6.26
Castleford	dep:	8.16	9.45	11.56	2.23	4.42	3.16	6.50
Methley Jc.	dep:	8.21	9.49	12.03	2.28	4.47	....	6.54
Methley MR	dep:	8.26	9.54	12.06	2.31	....	....	6.57
Leeds	arr:	8.42	10.15	12.23	2.46	5.08	3.34	7.15

In 1951 the service from Leeds to Knottingley had connections into trains between Wakefield and Goole at Knottingley, as follows, with the reverse of course applying. There was no Sunday service:

Leeds	dep: 5.20am	8.58	12.05pmSO	1.30	4.00*	5.35	6.35*	8.30
Castleford	dep: 5.44	9.25	12.32SO	1.57	4.27	6.02	7.02	8.57
Knottingley	arr: 5.54	9.36	12.42SO	2.07	4.37	6.12	7.12	9.08
Knottingley	dep: 7.54	9.47	12.58	2.30	4.53	6.18	7.16	9.20
Goole	arr: 8.24	10.17	1.28	3.02	5.25	6.53	7.46	9.51

Goole	dep: 5.39am	7.15	8.53	12.12pmSO	1.46	3.48	6.00	8.35
Knottingley	arr: 6.10	7.46	9.25	12.46	2.17	4.20	6.32	9.07
Knottingley	dep: 6.57	8.03	10.05	1.29	2.25	4.47	6.45	9.26
Castleford	dep: 7.08	8.15	10.16	1.40	2.38	5.00	6.58	9.37
								x
Leeds	arr: 7.38	8.44	10.46	2.10	3.11	5.31	7.26	10.00

* through trains   x then non-stop

No available photo of L & Y motive power at Castleford, so the next best thing is an 0.6.0 goods engine with a ballast train at Tanshelf in 1905.
Wakefield M.D.C. Leisure Services: Art Galleries and Museums

39

GN passenger services

The Methley Joint produced a pleasant crop of trains scuttling to and fro from either Leeds Central or Wakefield Westgate to Castleford, as in 1914:

Weekdays

Leeds	dep: 5.40am	....	9.05	10.28	12.08pm	1.32SO	....
Wakefield	dep:	6.48	....	....	....	....	2.00
Methley	dep: 6.08	7.05	9.36	11.50	12.37	1.59	2.16
Castleford	arr: 6.12	7.09	9.42	11.54	12.41	2.03	2.20

Leeds	dep: 4.24	5.03	6.18	7.27	10.00	10.28SO	10.50SO
Wakefield	dep:	....	....	....	....	....	....
Methley	dep: 4.30	5.39	6.47	8.16	10.23	10.45	11.16
Castleford	arr: 4.54	5.43	6.51	8.20	10.33	10.49	11.20

Sundays

Leeds	dep: 8.26am	9.35	2.52pm	3.40	8.14	....
Wakefield	dep:	....	....	....	....	8.06
Methley	dep: 8.56	10.50	3.17	4.39	8.42	8.21
Castleford	arr: 9.00	10.54	3.21	4.43	8.46	8.25

Weekdays

Castleford	dep: 8.15am	8.23	9.48	12.38pm	1.03	2.18SO	2.33
Methley	dep: 8.20	8.28	9.53	12.45	1.08	2.24	2.38
Wakefield	arr:	9.08	....	1.43	....	....	....
Leeds	arr: 8.48	....	10.23	....	1.36	2.53	3.37

Castleford	dep: 5.05	5.49	8.00	8.45	10.47	10.58SO	11.42
Methley	dep: 5.10	5.45	8.05	8.50	10.52	11.03	11.47
Wakefield	arr:	....	....	....	....	11.18	....
Leeds	arr: 5.38	7.14	8.34	9.28	11.20	....	12.13am

Sundays

Castleford	dep: 9.10am	12.05pm	3.30	4.55	8.35	9.10
Methley	dep: 9.15	12.10	3.35	5.00	8.40	9.15
Wakefield	arr:	....	....	5.20	9.17	....
Leeds	arr: 9.42	1.47	4.04	....	....	9.44

By 1951 the timetable appeared as follows, still with a good service on weekdays. Wakefield passengers changed at Ardsley.

Leeds Cen	dep:	5.20am	7.08	12.13pm	12.58SO	1.50	
Methley South	dep:	5.50	7.36	12.41	1.25	2.18	
Castleford	arr:	5.54	7.40	12.45	1.29	2.22	

Leeds Cen	dep:	2.45	4.18	5.20	5.47SX	6.20	10.15SO
Methley South	dep:	3.13	4.46	5.50	6.15	6.48	....
Castleford	arr	3.17	4.50	5.54	6.19	6.52	10.47

Castleford	dep:	6.37am	7.07	7.47	8.20	1.10pm	1.57SO
Methley South	dep:	6.42	7.12	....	....	1.15	2.02
Leeds Cen	arr:	7.00	7.40	8.20	8.51	1.44	2.31

Castleford	dep:	2.42	3.48	5.08	6.25	7.30	11.00SO
Methley South	dep:	2.47	3.53	5.13	6.30	7.35	....
Leeds Cen	arr:	3.16	4.22	5.42	6.59	8.04	11.31

N1 No. 69430 on a train to Leeds Cen. entering Methley Joint (South) station. Note the odd brake thirds in the formation. 9/4/55.   *J. P. Wilson*

N1 No. 69468 coasts into Castleford off the Methley Joint line. 7/9/53. J. P. Wilson

NER branch service

Next come the timetables for the Kippax branch, with the earlier, extended service to Pontefract as it was shown in 1914:

Leeds	dep:	6.50am	8.15	12.10pm	1.07SO	3.10
Ledstone	dep:	7.21	8.46	12.41	1.38	3.41
Castleford	dep:	7.26	8.53	12.48	1 43	3 43
Pontefract L & Y	arr:	....	9.02	12.57	....	3.57
Pontefract S & K	arr:	....	9.06	1.01	....	4.01

Leeds	dep:	6.08	9.28TuSO	10.30	11.30TuSO
Ledstone	dep:	6.39	10.07	11.09	12.10am
Castleford	dep:	6.46	10.12	11.14	12.16
Pontefract L & Y	arr:	6.55	....	....	....
Pontefract S & K	arr:	6.59	....	....	....

Pontefract S & K	dep:	....	9.25am	1.47pm	....	4.53
Pontefract L & Y	dep:	....	9.29	1.51	....	4.57
Castleford	dep:	7.58	9.38	1.59	2.29SO	5.05
Ledstone	dep:	8.04	9.44	2.05	2.35	5.11
Leeds	arr:	8.35	10.16	2.36	3.06	5.42

Pontefract S & K	dep:	7.40	....	....	....	....
Pontefract L & Y	dep:	7.44	....	....	....	....
Castleford	dep:	7.52	10.30TuSO	....	....	....
Ledstone	dep:	7.58	10.36	....	....	....
Leeds	arr:	8.31	11.07	....	....	....

There were no Sunday trains. TuSO-Tuesdays and Saturdays only.

By 1949 the service had been reduced to three on weekdays only. Ledston had lost its 'e' in the timetable:

Miles

Miles							
0	Castleford	dep:	6.55amSO	7.00SX	9.48	4.50pmSX	7.25
2¼	Ledston	dep:	7.01	7.06	9.54	4.56	7.31
3¼	Bowers	dep:	7.06	7.11	9.59	5.01	7.36
4	Kippax	dep:	7.11	7.15	10.03	5.05	7.40
7	Garforth	dep:	7.19	7.23	10.13	5.13	7.51
9¾	Crossgates	dep:	7.25	7.29	10.19	5.19	7.57
11½	Osmondthorpe	dep:	7.29	7.33	10.23	....	8.01
13½	Marsh Lane	dep:	7.34	7.41	10.31	....	8.09
14¼	Leeds City	arr:	7.37	7.41	10.31	5.28	8.09

Leeds City	dep:	8.10am	3.40pm	6.15
Marsh Lane	dep:	8.13	3.43	6.19
Osmondthorpe	dep:	8.18	3.48	6.24
Crossgates	dep:	8.23	3.53	6.30
Garforth	dep:	8.29	3.59	6.36
Kippax	dep:	8.35	4.05	6.42
Bowers	dep:	8.38	4.08	6.45
Ledston	dep:	8.42	4.12	6.49
Castleford	arr:	8.47	4.17	6.54

Although the service was a basic one, it still managed to be more ragged in one direction than in the other, with an odd morning train out from Castleford added to three out and home trains from Leeds.

Lettered 'Manchester London Road Push & Pull' this set is seeing out its days on Leeds-Castleford trains via the Methley Joint. All manner of vintage stock was to be seen in the West Riding in the early 1950s. An ex-GCR C13 4.4.2T may well have been on the other end. *R. G. Rockett Collection*

V2. No. 60863 pauses at Castleford with the 7.40pm to York on 9/7/50.
R. G. Rocket Collection

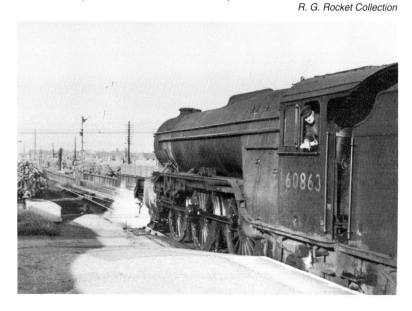

No. 56125 passing Ledston Station with 7K83 Bowers Row-Drax. The site has
hardly improved with time. 29/10/85. S. Batty

-Last but not least, NER main line trains

Trains along the axis running from east to west undoubtedly would
provide the most interesting motive power and spectacle, with two main
streams, namely those running between Hull, Selby and Normanton and
the eastern thrust of the L & Y from Liverpool and Manchester towards
York and Newcastle, whose expresses nearly all called at Normanton and
Castleford.

Firstly, then, an idea of things in 1914:

Weekdays

Halifax	dep:	....	8.43	....	1.58	....	5.40	....	...
Normanton	dep:	7.12am	9.24	12.07pm	2.49	5.30	6.19	7.50	9.30
Castleford	dep:	7.20	9.31	12.14	2.56	5.38	6.26	7.57	9.38
Selby	dep:	8.18	10.10	1.02	3.31	6.16	7.00	9.08	10.48
						x			
Hull	arr:	9.24	10.57	....	4.10	6.56	7.35	10.13	11.39

Sundays

Normanton	dep: 3.10am	7.55	2.10pm	7.00
Castleford	dep:	8.03	....	7.08
Selby	dep: 3.45	9.04	2.45	8.09
Hull	arr: 4.42	10.09	3.25	9.14

x - change at Monk Fryston

Weekdays

Hull	dep: 8.55am	11.00	....	3.20	....	....	8.40
Selby	dep: 9.48	11.54	2.54pm	4.12	6.20	8.15	9.18
Castleford	dep:10.16	12.19	4.17	4.35	7.06	9.00	9.50
Normanton	dep:10.23	12.25	4.24	4.42	7.13	9.07	9.57
Halifax	arr:11.10	1.11	....	5.25	....	....	....

Sundays

Hull	dep: 6.50am	....	8.05
Selby	dep: 7.56	6.57pm	9.23
Castleford	dep: 8.56	8.05	9.50
Normanton	dep: 9.02	8.12	9.57

A short load for B1 No. 61383 on a Wakefield - York train at Whitwood Jc. 24/4/55.
J. P. Wilson

It is interesting to compare the tables with what was on offer in Summer 1949:

	Weekdays		Sundays		Weekdays	
Normanton	dep: 7.15am	4.20am	9.25pm	Selby	dep:	9.58am
Castleford	dep: 7.29	4.30	9.34	Castleford	dep:	10.21
Selby	arr: 8.47	4.56	9.55	Normanton	arr:	10.54

There were seven L & Y expresses between Liverpool, Manchester and York, with two extended to Newcastle. All of these stopped at Castleford in 1914, providing a superior service:

Weekdays

Liverpool Exch	dep:	....	....	....	10.50	....	....
Manchester Vic	dep:	....	7.00am	....	....	....	12.25
Normanton	dep:	7.12	9.02	11.40am	12.07pm	1.04	2.49
Castleford	dep:	7.20am	9.10	11.50	12.14	1.13	2.56
York	arr:	8.15	9.46	12.16	1.08	1.42	3.54
		*			**		
Newcastle	arr:	....	....	....	....	3.48	.... '

'Jubilee' No. 45569 'Gwalior' on arrival at Castleford on a Summer Saturday working from Blackpool. August 1964. R. G. Rockett

Liverpool Exch	dep:	....	....	....	6.40	....
Manchester Vic	dep:	3.50	....	....	....	....
Normanton	dep:	5.30	6.55	7.50	9.30	11.00
Castleford	dep:	5.38	7.05	7.57	9.38	11.09
York	arr:	6.29	7.32	9.01	10.12	11.36
		*				

Newcastle	arr:	....	....	....	12.37am	....

Newcastle	dep:	....	....	....	12.30pm	....	....
York	dep:	6.45am	9.57	12.13pm	2.35	1.36	3.25
Castleford	dep:	7.37	10.28	12.43	3.04	2.27	4.17
Normanton	dep:	7.45	10.35	....	3.10	2.34	4.24
		*				*	*

Manchester Vic	arr:	....	12.13	2.07	....	....	....
Liverpool Exch	arr:	....	....	....	5.10	....	....

Newcastle	dep:	....	....	....	....
York	dep:	4.25	6.15	6.45	8.08
Castleford	dep:	4.45	7.06	7.18	9.00
Normanton	dep:	5.02	7.13	7.25	9.07
			*	*	*

Manchester Vic	arr:	....	....	....	....
Liverpool Exch	arr:	7.48	....	....	....

Sundays

Normanton	dep:	7.55am	4.29pm	7.00	York	dep:	7.55am	10.35	7.00pm
Castleford	dep:	8.03	4.40	7.08	Castleford	dep:	8.56	11.01	8.05
York	arr:	9.05	5.15	8.08	Normanton	arr:	9.03	11.10	8.12
		*	x				*	xx	

* all stations.   x leaves Liverpool Exch at 1.15pm
                      xx arrives Liverpool Exch at 2.54pm.

1949 offered not so many trains, but they were probably more interesting for the observer:

Liverpool Exch	dep:	....	....	....	....	10.25SO
Manchester Vic	dep:	....	....	1.08	12.10pmSO	....
Normanton	dep:	7.15am	8.55	11.53	1.52	1.02
Castleford	dep:	7.29	9.06	12.01	2.01	1.09
York	arr:	8.15	9.40	12.28	2.28	1.36
			a			b

Liverpool Exch	dep:	....	....	6.35
Manchester Vic	dep:	....	....	....
Normanton	dep:	5.30SO	7.06	9.35
Castleford	dep:	5.49	7.15	9.44
York	arr:	6.30	7.48	10.15
			c	

a to Scarborough Cen. arr 11.00. b arr. Newcastle 4.12. c from Blackpool North

Scarborough	dep:	....	....	11.45SO	....	....
York	dep:	6.45SO	10.15	12.50pm	2.00	2.45SO
Castleford	dep:	7.37	10.47	1.22	2.30	3.33
Normanton	dep:	7.45	10.54	....	2.38	3.41
Manchester Vic	arr:	....	12.46	....	....	....
Liverpool Exch	arr:	....	....	....	5.18	....
		a	b	x		

Scarborough	dep:	....	....	....	7.25	7.25
York	dep:	....	5.12	7.08	8.35FX	8.42FO
Castleford	dep:	4.22SO	5.46	7.38	9.22	9.32
Normanton	dep:	....	5.52	7.45	8.29	9.40
Manchester Vic	arr:	....	7.39	....	....	....
Liverpool Exch	arr:	....	....	10.43	....	....
		c		d		

a - to Blackpool North b - to Blackpool North SO x - to Bradford Exch.
c - from Bridlington to Bradford Exch. d - from Newcastle. FX - Except
Fridays. FO - Fridays Only.

Sundays

Normanton	:	7.56am	1.05pm	4.20	7.25
Castleford	:	8.07	1.15	4.30	7.34
York	:	8.40	1.42	5.25	8.07
		a	b	aa	

a - from Wakefield Westgate aa - from Wakefield and via Selby b - from
Liverpool Exch.

York	:	11.25am	5.15pm	7.05	9.25
Castleford	:	11.57	5.52	7.38	9.56
Normanton	:	12.05	5.59	7.46	10.04
		w		d	w

w - to Wakefield Westgate d - to Liverpool Exch.

Minor contenders

Prior to Grouping in 1923, when almost all the smaller groups of railway companies were merged into four large ones, the Hull & Barnsley railway, a smallish concern which was fiercely independent of its brash local competitor, the North Eastern, arranged its service of trains, of which there were, alas, not many, to connect with L & Y services at Knottingley for connections to Leeds over the Methley branch, a procedure which lasted from 1885 up to the wartime restrictions of 1917. In 1910 the timetable appeared as follows:

Hull Cannon St.	dep:	7.00am	12.30pm	5.00	
Carlton	dep:	8.52	1.35	6.00	
Knottingley	arr:	9.10	1.52	6.17	
Knottingley	dep:	9.35	2.13	6.34	
Leeds	arr:	10.15	2.34	7.11	

Leeds	dep:	9.10am	10.45	1.25pm	5.42
Knottingley	arr:	9.43	11.18	1.58	6.16
Knottingley	dep:	9.37	12.37	2.20	7.45
Carlton	dep:	10.15	12.55	2.38	8.01
Hull Cannon St.	arr:	11.40	....	4.10	9.18

Even more enterprising were the H & B 'Cook's Excursions' on Saturdays from Hull to Leeds by the same route and bringing Stirling's 'invisible green' domeless engines through Methley Jc. The trains usually left Cannon Street at 1.00pm and arrived in Leeds at 2.32, with the return at 10.45pm, one hour later for pantomimes. The return in Cannon Street was at 12.17am or the corresponding hour later. The fare for the outing was 2/(10p). Football excursions also ran on the same direction, the 0-6-0 or perhaps the bigger 4-4-0 running non-stop to Carlton where a halt was made for water, then taking up an L & Y pilotman at Knottingley for the run to a West Riding venue, perhaps Bradford or Huddersfield. Thus, another company's rolling stock was seen at Methley.

Tramcars and Industrials

A short word on the tramways around Castleford. The turn of the century brought along the efficient though much slower electric tramways, with the West Riding tramways, the forerunner of the West Riding Omnibus Company operating on a long route out of Wakefield through Stanley, across the railway bridge above Normanton station and then following a straight course of three miles north east to Castleford NE station, reached via Lumley, Oxford and Cambridge streets. The line was double track along the first two. The line then turned northwards up Station road to turn east into Carlton street and then south into Bridge street under the railway for the run to Pontefract. Another route came in from the Methley direction along Albion street, then diverging either along Carlton street or keeping near to the river along Church and Aire streets before turning south to join the route in Bridge street. The 1908 survey also gives a route off the Methley line running directly south to Cutsyke station, where it terminated. In Pontefract the line passed Monkhill and Tanshelf stations, reaching Knottingley by way of the station at that place. All in all, then, a pretty sharp competitor for local traffic. The whole of this

50

local system, which offered a certain amount of headache to the railway companies, was a little over 25 miles in length. The Normanton-Castleford-Pontefract section was in fact isolated from the main system and was abandoned in 1925, all Wakefield routes going in 1932. The total number of cars in the fleet was 75.

There were two industrial branches at Castleford, both off the NER line on its northern side. The first was a longish one of 74 chains running north east from Whitwood Jc. off a headshunt, single track and crossing the Methley road by a skew viaduct to reach, in order, a hearthrug works, furniture works and pottery, finally ending up at a large chemical works by the Aire. All this activity except the last was at the north side of the line.

Beyond the station to the east and near the site of the old station a shorter line of 29 chains turned northwards out of a headshunt of three sidings. After crossing Wheldon road it encountered three gasholders before diving to serve a tar depot, a rye bread factory and, presumably, its raison d'etre, another large chemical works by the river. This line was also single. By way of interest, between this line and the Kippax branch which took off further east was the football ground.

Near Moss street on the Whitwood branch were at one time at set of sidings.

The first car to leave Castleford for Pontefract, with admirers.   *Castleford Library*

Aire Street. Castleford c. 1910.
Wakefield M.D.C. Leisure Services: Art Galleries and Museums

Firms registered with the Railway Clearing House for Traffic in 1930

Aire & Calder Chemical Works. (Hunt Bros).
Aire & Calder Glass Bottle Works.
Anlgo-American Oil Company.
Austin Bros.
Bellamy's Confectionery.
Castleford Flint Glass Bottle Company.
T.P. Fawcett.
Hickson & Partners.
Clokie & Company.
Healdfield Brickworks. (J. Hartley & Co.)
High Town Glass Bottle Works.
J. Lumb's Glass Bottle Works.
Red Hill Brick Works.
Ridge Field Brick Company.
Yorkshire Brick Company Ltd.

Firms registered with the Railway Clearing House cont.

Airedale Colliery.
Glasshoughton Colliery.
W. Morris Ltd.
Pope & Pearson Collieries
Whitwood Collieries.
Yorkshire Coking & Chemical Co.

Miscellaneous signalling and working instructions

List of signal boxes in the Castleford area

Distance between
locations

0 000yd.	Altofts Jc. LMS & NE Joint.
0 757 yd.	West Riding Colliery frame. (Down line)
1 791yd.	Whitwood Jc.
0 424yd.	Moss Street frame. (Down line)
0 935yd.	Castleford Gates.
0 506yd.	Castleford Station.
0 866yd.	Castleford Old Station.
0 686yd.	Wheldale.
0 502yd.	Wheldale Colliery frame. (Down line)
0 1351yd.	Fryston South.
0 629yd.	Fryston North.
1 443yd.	Burton Salmon.
1 1719yd.	Monk Fryston.
0 000yd.	Castleford Old Station.
1 1215yd.	Ledston.
1 133yd.	Allerton Main.
0 924yd.	Kippax Yard frame. (Facing to Down trains)
0 262yd.	Kippax.
2 855yd.	Garforth Trench Pit frame.
0 366yd.	Garforth.

Distance between
locations

0 000yd.	Cutsyke LMS.
0 433yd.	Ridgefield frame.
0 440yd.	Castleford.

Special routing whistles for action by the signalman at:

Whitwood Jc.	3 short for freight trains requiring No. 1 Up Goods line at Altofts. Jc. 1 short for freight trains requiring No. 2 Up Goods line at Altofts Jc.
Castleford Station.	2 short. for freight trains having to detach at Castleford. 1 long. 3 short for freight trains having to stop at Wheldale colliery.
Fryston South.	1 long for Cutsyke branch at Castleford Station. 2 short for detaching at Whitwood colliery. 3 short for detaching at West Riding colliery. 4 short for detaching at Whitwood and West Riding or Moss Street. 1 short. 1 long for Ardsley direction.
Burton Salmon.	1 short for freight trains detaching at Castleford Gates. 4 short for freight trains for Garforth branch. 1 short. 2 long for freight trains requiring water at Castleford.
Castleford Gates.	1 long. 2 short for Down Yard to Lumb's New Yard. 2 short. 1 long for Down Yard to Lumb's High Town Siding. 2 short for No. 1 Group to Down Main. 2 short. 1 crow for No. 1 Group to Up Main. 4 short for No. 1 or No. 2 Group to Shunting Neck. 3 short for No. 2 Group to Down Main. 3 short. 1 crow for No. 2 Group to Up Main.

Special Instructions for Drivers in the LNER Working Appendix for 1947

Whitwood Branch. The normal position of the Pottery Street level crossing gates is across the line, and Drivers when approaching must sound the engine whistle to inform the Siding Foreman that the level crossing gates require to be reversed. East Branch. On the Down journey the train must stop at the Wheldale road bridge until the Driver receives a hand signal from the crossing keeper that all is clear at the level crossing, and also an all-right signal from the assistant guard.

The assistant guard must precede the train from Wheldale road bridge to see that the points are right and the line clear in the yard. Engine to be in front and guard's van in rear in both directions. Engines of classes J 71 or J 72 only must be used and must in all cases go down bunker first. The speed must not exceed four miles per hour.

Messrs. Clokie's Siding, Moss Street. Traffic, loaded or empty, for this siding must be placed in position clear of the gate on the east side of Pottery street. Traffic from this siding will be placed by Messrs. Clokie's people at the same point, ready for removal by LNER engines.

Wagons must not be propelled on to be the sidings or drawn out over the level crossing.

Kippax: Working trains into and out of Allerton Main Colliery sidings.

Working Appendix. June 1931.

The Signalman at Allerton Main Colliery, whenever possible, must inform the Guard and Driver of trains going into the colliery if another train or engine is likely to enter the colliery line before their train is ready to depart. Guards of trains working into Allerton Main colliery sidings must observe the following instructions:

Trains propelled from Allerton Main Colliery Box: After the train is stopped at the entrance to the colliery sidings for the purpose of detaching the engine, the brakes on one or two wagons must be pinned down before the engine is detached. The wagons may then be allowed to gravitate into the colliery yard, the Guard pinning down a sufficient number of brakes to prevent the train from getting out of control.

Before a train is allowed to leave the colliery sidings for Allerton Main Colliery Box, the Guard must inform the Signalman by means of the telephone provided near the Weigh Office, that the train is ready to leave, and the Guard must not give the necessary hand signal for the train to leave the sidings until the branch Up Outer Home signal has been lowered.

For shunting purposes engines may leave the colliery sidings and travel towards the Branch Up Outer Home signal after it has been ascertained by the Guard that no train is approaching from the junction and it is safe to do so.

Enginemen and Guards must keep a sharp look out when travelling between Allerton Main Colliery Box and the colliery sidings, and be prepared to stop if there is any obstruction on the single line.

Owing to the gradient of the line, trains working traffic into and out of the sidings must always have the engine at the lower (Ledston) end, or the whole of the trains must be placed in the sidings clear of the Main line before any shunting operations are begun. Under no circumstances must the van, wagons or any portion of the train be left on the Main line during the time the engine is in the sidings.

Kippax: Working of Traffic into and out of the Siding: When trains from the direction of Castleford have traffic to attach or detach in this Siding, the portion of train left on the Main line must be securely held by the van brake being put hard on, and in addition the brakes of two wagons on the portion of train left on the Main line must also be pinned down. All wagons to be attached to the train must be set back with the engine coupled to them and must come up to the standing train as gently as possible.

Important dates for Collieries in the area
(Supplied by Ron. Rockett)

Fryston	Produced first coal 1874	Closed end 1985
Glasshoughton	Opened 1869	Closed 1986
Glasshoughton Coke Ovens	Opened 1912	Closed 1979
Whitwood	Opened 1840	Closed early 1969
Wheldale	Opened 1870	Closed 1988(?)
Primrose Hill	Opened 1893	Closed late 1969
Allerton Bywater	Opened originally 1700, then 1875	Due to close 1992
West Riding Colliery	Opened 1851. Last coal drawn 1966	Main shaft closed 1962.

R 2460 (H.D?)

EXCURSION

TO

SCARBOROUGH

(LONDESBOROUGH ROAD)

SUNDAY, 27th JULY

OUTWARD			Return Fares Third Class		RETURN		
		a.m.	s.	d.			p.m.
Castleford (N.E.R.)	... dep.	9*30	8	0	Scarborough (L. Rd.)	... dep.	7 10
Burton Salmon ...	... ,,	9 40	7	9			
Sherburn-in-Elmet ...	... ,,	9 50	7	3	Sherburn-in-Elmet	... arr.	8 22
					Burton Salmon ...	... ,,	8 31
Scarborough (L. Rd.) .	... arr.	11 2	—		Castleford (N.E.R.)	.. ,,	8*42

PASSENGERS RETURN SAME DAY ONLY AS SHOWN

---

* SPECIAL BUS ARRANGEMENTS

The West Riding Automobile Company will provide facilities to and from Castleford Station by ordinary service and special buses in connection with this excursion. The buses being operated as shown below :—

TO CASTLEFORD STATION		Dep. a.m.	Single Bus Fare	RETURN ARRANGEMENTS
Airedale Hotel	...	8 54	4d.	
Magnet Hotel	...	8 57	4d.	Ordinary Service buses can be obtained to all the above
Fryston Road End	...	9 0	4d.	points.
Mickletown (Queen's Hotel) ...		8 51	4d.	
Mickletown (Saville Pit)	...	8 55	4d.	
Pinfold Lane (Leeds Road end) ...		9 0	4d.	
Three Lane Ends	...	9 5	2d.	

Children under three years of age, free ; three years and under fourteen, half-fares

Tickets can be obtained IN ADVANCE at Stations and accredited rail ticket Agencies

Further information will be supplied on application to Stations, Enquiry Offices, Agencies, Mr. T. W. Poling, District Passenger Superintendent, City Station, Leeds, Tel. 31711 (Ext. 269), or to Mr. H. E. Richardson, District Commercial Superintendent, York, Tel. 53022 (Ext. 397)

CONDITIONS

These tickets are issued subject to the conditions of issue of ordinary passenger tickets where applicable, and also to the special conditions as set out in the Bye-Laws, Regulations and Conditions in the Published Notices of the Railway Executive LUGGAGE ALLOWANCES as set out in these published notices.

Published by the Railway Executive (N.E. Region) 7/52   Printed in Gt. Britain   RE1879—Petty & Sons Ltd., Leeds—C1

METRO · TRAIN Goole and Hallam Lines

Leeds - Castleford - Knottingley-Goole / Barnsley - Sheffield

1 October 1990 until 12 May 1991

Mondays to Saturdays

Leeds – Goole section

Station		BHX SX	BHX SX	SX	SO	SX		BHX		BHX SX	BHX		
Leeds	d.	0528	0559	0633	0639	0707	0754	0812	0825	0907	0934	1007	1034
Woodlesford	d.	0538	0608	0642	0648	0716	0803	0821	0834	0916	0943	1016	1043
Castleford	a.	0549	0618	0652	0658	0726	0813	0831	0844	0926	0954	1026	1054
Castleford	d.	0551	0620	0654	0700	0732	0815	0833	0846	0928	0956	1028	1056
Pontefract Monkhill	d.		0627					0840		0939		1035	
Knottingley	d.		06a33					08a46		09a41		10a41	
Whitley Bridge	d.												
Hensall	d.												
Snaith	d.												
Rawcliffe	d.												
Goole	a.												

Normanton – Sheffield section

Normanton	d.	0558	0659	0705	0737	0820	0851		1001	1101
Wakefield Kirkgate	d.	0603	0705	0711	07b48	0827	0857	0916	1007	1107
Darton	d.	0616	0716	0722	0759	0838	0908	0929	1018	1118
Barnsley	a.	0624	0722	0728	0805	0844	0914	0936	1024	1124
Wombwell	a.	0630	0727	0736	0814	0851	0928	0943	1030	1130
Elsecar	a.	0634	0730	0739	0817	0854	0931	0946	1033	1133
Chapeltown	a.	0640	0735	0744	0822	0859	0936	0953	1038	1138
Meadowhall	a.	0646	0741	0750	0828	0905	0941	0959	1044	1144
Brightside	a.	0649			0830					
Attercliffe	a.	0653	0746	0755	0833					
Sheffield	a.	0659	0752	0801	0839	0914	0950	1008	1053	1152

Leeds – Goole section

Station		BHX		†		BHX				BHX				BHX
Leeds	d.	1107	1134	1207	1234	1307	1334	1407	1434	1507	1534	1607	1634	1708
Woodlesford	d.	1116	1143	1216	1243	1316	1343	1416	1443	1516	1543	1616	1643	1718
Castleford	a.	1126	1154	1226	1254	1327	1354	1426	1454	1526	1554	1626	1654	1727
Castleford	d.	1128	1156	1228	1256		1356	1428	1456	1528	1556	1628	1656	1732
Pontefract Monkhill	d.	1135		1235				1435		1535		1635		
Knottingley	d.	11a41		1239				14a41		15a41		16a41		
Whitley Bridge	d.			1246										
Hensall	d.			1249										
Snaith	d.			1255										
Rawcliffe	d.			1300										
Goole	a.			1311										

Normanton – Sheffield section

Normanton	d.	1201	1301	1401	1501	1601	1701	1738
Wakefield Kirkgate	d.	1207	1307	1407	1507	1607	1707	1744
Darton	d.	1218	1318	1418	1518	1618	1718	1757
Barnsley	a.	1224	1324	1424	1524	1624	1724	1805
Wombwell	a.	1230	1330	1430	1530	1630	1735	1821
Elsecar	a.	1233	1333	1433	1533	1633	1738	1824
Chapeltown	a.	1238	1338	1438	1538	1638	1743	1831
Meadowhall	a.	1244	1344	1444	1544	1644	1749	1837
Brightside	a.							
Attercliffe	a.						1754	
Sheffield	a.	1252	1353	1452	1554	1655	1800	1848

Notes: a Arrive. d Depart.
b Arrives 0742. BHX Will not run on Bank Holidays, 1 January, 1 April and 6 May 1991.
SX Saturdays excepted. SO Saturdays only.
† Will terminate at or start from Knottingley on Bank Holidays, 1 January, 1 April and 6 May 1991.
The information shown is subject to alteration on Public Holidays. Please check before travelling.

01.10.90

METRO·TRAIN Goole and Hallam Lines.

Mondays to Saturdays

Station		1	2	3	4	5	6	7	8	9	10	11	12	13
		BHX			SO	SX	BHX					BHX		
Leeds	d	1722	1740	1810	1837	1841	1907	1937	2007	2036	2107	2136	2207	2236
Woodlesford	d	1731	1749	1819	1846	1850	1916	1946	2016	2045	2116	2145	2216	2245
Castleford	a	1741	1758	1829	1855	1859	1926	1955	2026	2054	2126	2154	2226	2254
Castleford	d	1743	1800	1831	1857	1901	1928	1957	2028	2056	2128	2156	2228	2256
Pontefract Monkhill	d	1750		1838			1935		2035		2135		2235	
Knottingley	a	1755		1844			1941		2041		2141		2241	
Whitley Bridge	d	1801												
Hensall	d	1806												
Snaith	d	1812												
Rawcliffe	d	1817												
Goole	a	1830												
Normanton	d		1806		1903	1907		2003		2102		2202		2302
Wakefield Kirkgate	d		1812		1909	1913		2009		2108		2208		2308
Darton	d		1823		1920	1924		2020		2119		2219		2319
Barnsley	a		1828		1925	1929		2025		2124		2224		2324
Wombwell	a				1931	1935		2031		2130		2230		2330
Elsecar	a				1935	1938		2034		2134		2234		2334
Chapeltown	a				1940	1943		2039		2139		2239		2339
Meadowhall Interchange	a		1846		1950	1950		2046		2145		2245		2345
Sheffield	a		1854		1958	1958		2057		2153		2253		2353

Station		1	2	3	4	5	6	7	8	9	10	11	12	13
		SX		SX	SX●									
Sheffield	d	0535	0606		0640		0706	0810		0910		1010		1110
Meadowhall Interchange	d	0541	0614		0647		0715	0816		0916		1016		1116
Chapeltown	d	0547	0620		0653		0721	0822		0922		1022		1122
Elsecar	d	0552	0625		0658		0726	0827		0927		1027		1127
Wombwell	d	0555	0629		0702		0729	0830		0930		1030		1130
Barnsley	d	0601	0635		0708		0735	0836		0936		1036		1136
Darton	d	0607	0640		0714		0741	0842		0942		1042		1142
Wakefield Kirkgate	d	0619	0652		0726		0753	0854		0954		1054		1154
Normanton	d	0623	0657		0731		0757	0858		0958		1058		1158
Goole	d					0710								
Rawcliffe	d					0717								
Snaith	d					0722								
Hensall	d					0728								
Whitley Bridge	d					0732								
Knottingley	d			0704		0741			0921		1021		1121	
Pontefract Monkhill	d			0708		0745			0925		1025		1125	
Castleford	a	0630	0703	0715	0737	0752	0803	0904	0932	1004	1032	1104	1135	1204
Castleford	d	0632	0705	0718	0739	0755	0805	0906	0935	1006	1035	1106	1137	1206
Woodlesford	d	0643	0716	0729	0749	0809	0816	0917	0946	1017	1046	1117	1148	1217
Leeds	a	0654	0728	0743	0801	0820	0829	0930	0959	1028	1058	1128	1159	1230

Notes: a Arrive. d Depart.

BHX Will not run on Bank Holiday Monday, 26 August 1991.

SX Saturdays excepted. SO Saturdays only

For details of other trains between Barnsley and Sheffield see SYPTE timetable.

The information shown is subject to alteration especially during Public Holidays. Please check before travelling.

● Also calls at Attercliffe Road.

METRO·TRAIN Goole and Hallam Lines.

Mondays to Saturdays

			BHX		△		BHX			BHX ◆		◆	BHX SX●
Sheffield	d		1210		1310		1410		1510		1607		1710	1755
Meadowhall Interchange	d		1216		1316		1416		1516		1616		1719	1802
Chapeltown	d		1222		1322		1422		1522		1622		1725	1808
Elsecar	d		1227		1327		1427		1527		1627		1730	1814
Wombwell	d		1230		1330		1430		1530		1630		1733	1817
Barnsley	d		1236		1336		1436		1536		1636		1739	1823
Darton	d		1242		1342		1442		1542		1642		1745	1829
Wakefield Kirkgate	d		1254		1354		1454		1554		1654		1757	1841
Normanton	d		1258		1358		1458		1558		1658		1801	1846
Goole	d					1352								
Rawcliffe	d					1359								
Snaith	d					1404								
Hensall	d					1410								
Whitley Bridge	d					1414								
Knottingley	d	1221				1421		1521		1621		1721		
Pontefract Monkhill	d	1225				1425		1525		1625		1725		
Castleford	a	1232	1304		1404	1435	1504	1532	1604	1632	1704	1734	1807	1852
Castleford	d	1235	1306	1335	1406	1437	1506	1535	1606	1635	1706	1736	1809	1854
Woodlesford	d	1246	1317	1346	1417	1448	1517	1546	1617	1646	1717	1747	1820	1904
Leeds	a	1258	1328	1358	1429	1459	1530	1558	1628	1659	1729	1802	18g35	1917

				△		BHX		BHX	●
Sheffield	d	1812		1910		2010		2110	2210
Meadowhall Interchange	d	1818		1916		2016		2116	2217
Chapeltown	d	1824		1922		2022		2122	2223
Elsecar	d	1829		1927		2027		2127	2229
Wombwell	d	1832		1930		2030		2130	2232
Barnsley	d	1838		1936		2036		2136	2238
Darton	d	1844		1942		2042		2142	2243
Wakefield Kirkgate	d	1856		1954		2054		2154	2255
Normanton	d	1900		1958		2058		2158	2300
Goole	d		1852						
Rawcliffe	d		1859						
Snaith	d		1904						
Hensall	d		1910						
Whitley Bridge	d		1914						
Knottingley	d		1921		2021		2121		2221	2300
Pontefract Monkhill	d		1925		2025		2125		2225	2304
Castleford	a	1906	1932	2004	2032	2104	2132	2204	2232	2306	2311
Castleford	d	1908	1935	2006	2035	2106	2135	2206	2235	2308	2314
Woodlesford	d	1919	1946	2017	2046	2117	2146	2217	2246	2318	2325
Leeds	a	1931	1957	2028	2057	2128	2202	2228	2302	2330	2336

Notes: a Arrive. d Depart. g Saturdays arrives 1831

BHX Will not run on Bank Holiday Monday, 26 August 1991

SX Saturdays excepted

For details of other trains between Barnsley and Sheffield see SYPTE timetable

The information shown is subject to alteration especially during Public Holidays. Please check before travelling.

● Also calls at Attercliffe Road.

△ Will start from Knottingley on Bank Holiday Monday, 26 August 1991

◆ Also calls at Brightside and Attercliffe Road.

B(HD)771

HALIFAX v CASTLEFORD

KICK OFF 2.15 P.M.

FOOTBALL EXCURSION

TO

HALIFAX

SATURDAY DECEMBER 31st

OUTWARD JOURNEY		Return fares third class	RETURN JOURNEY	
	p.m.	s. d.		p.m.
Castleford .. .. .. dep.	12 5	3 0	Halifax (Old).. .. .. dep.	4 50
Methley (Eastern Region) .. „	12 11	2 9		
Stanley.. .. .. .. „	12 18	2 6	Stanley .. .. .. arr.	5 56
			Methley (Eastern Region) „	6 4
Halifax (Old) .. .. arr.	1 15	—	Castleford .. .. .. „	6 10

PASSENGERS RETURN THE SAME DAY ONLY AS SHOWN ABOVE

Tickets can be obtained IN ADVANCE at stations and agencies

Further information will be supplied on application to stations, offices, agencies, or to G. B. Gray, District Passenger Manager, Central station, Leeds, Tel: 31711 (Ext. 395), or C. Dandridge, Commercial Superintendent, Liverpool Street station, London E.C.2, Tel: BIShopsgate 7600

Published by The Railway Executive (Eastern Region)   Printed in Gt. Britain   3075—John Waddington Ltd., Leeds—1,000

Garforth and Scarborough. Guaranteed Day Excursion.

Saturday, 5th. July 1924.

Kippax Central Working Men's Club. (Two trains)

Garforth	dep:	6.05am	6.15am
Garforth Inner Jc.	pass:	6.07	6.20
Kippax	arr:		6.25
	dep:	6.15	6.30
Bowers Coll Jc.	pass:	6.19	6.35
Ledston	arr:		6.40
	dep:	6.23	6.44
Castleford Inner Jc.	pass:	6.28	6.50
Castleford	arr:	6.32	6.55
	dep:	6.41	7.04
Milford Jc.	pass:	6.53	7.16
Church Fenton	pass:	7.00	7.25
York	pass:	7.17	7.45
Malton (water)	arr:	7.50	8.18
	dep:	7.55	8.23
Washbeck Exc. Plat.	arr:	8.27	8.55
Washbeck Exc. Plat.	dep:	10.10pm	10.20pm
Malton (water)	arr:	10.43	10.53
	dep:	10.48	10.58
York	pass	11.20	11.30
Church Fenton	pass:	11.36	11.46
Milton Jc.	pass:	11.43	11.53
Castleford	arr:	11.54	12.06am
	dep:	12.03am	12.15
Castleford Inner Jc.	pass:	12.05	12.17
Ledston	dep:	12.10	12.21
Kippax	dep:	12.18	12.29
Garforth	arr:	12.24	12.35

NOTES